50 THINGS TO DO WHEN YOU TURN 50

Riley Lucero

Bridge Press

support@bridgepress.org

Please consider writing a review!

Just visit: <u>purplelink.org/review</u>

ISBN: 978-1-955149-24-2

TABLE OF CONTENTS

INTRODUCTION

So, it finally happened. You turned 50. The big five-oh. Over the hill. Half a century. Depending on when you're reading this, that means that you were most likely alive for the fall of the Berlin Wall and September 11. You possibly even remember when President Richard Nixon resigned following the Watergate scandal. Considering that most of those experiences are now referenced primarily in history books, you should be proud that you have a firsthand understanding of certain events that changed the course of history itself.

But knowing that doesn't make you any happier to be turning 50, does it? If you're like most of the 13,000 people who will turn 50 on any given day, you're trying to juggle a healthy dose of optimism about the future, satisfaction with the past, and a few question marks about to how to spend the next 30 or 40 (or more!) years of your life.

You're probably also plagued with a whole new host of health concerns, some of which you've never even considered before. For instance, now that you're officially "over the hill," you have to start thinking about when you should schedule your first colonoscopy, as well as taking recommendations for lawyers to help you with estate planning. Sounds fun, doesn't it?

While none of these are exciting prospects, they don't have to be complete mysteries. I wrote this book primarily to provide some guidance about this very uncertain time in your life. But more than that, this is a guide to help you create a plan for moving forward. In my experience — both for myself and from talking to others — the question of "What's next?" is usually the most nerve-racking part of it. After all, you're usually too young to think about retiring, but you're also generally too old to consider a career change.

Or are you? Without borrowing the obnoxious cliché that "50 is the new 40" or anything similar, you should take heart in knowing that 50-year-olds are more capable, active, and prepared to enter the second half of their life than ever before. Enormous leaps in healthcare and technology have created a world in which 50-year-olds not only exist well, but thrive. So, take heart. Every indication is that the next several decades will be very kind to you.

Regardless of how you plan for the future, the absolute worst thing that you can do is try to recapture what life was like when you were younger. I've seen too many 55-year-old empty-nesters that have tried to bring back a hairstyle or a pair of acid-washed jeans from the '80s, and it looks as ridiculous as you think it would.

Moreover, your body isn't the same as it used to be, either. Embrace that; don't run from it. This new stage of your life is exciting and filled with optimism, but it all depends on how you approach it.

In the pages to follow, we've lined up 50 things that you should do or plan for, now that you're 50 years old. Some of them are health related and some of them are meant to be pondered while you're sitting on the back porch with a glass of ice-cold tea in your hand. Others are things you can look forward to (which almost seems scary now that the end might be more firmly in view).

Don't let it worry you. Think of the last 50 years as a dress rehearsal for what can now be the most exciting time of your life. You have wisdom, resources, and time on your side to make all the dreams of your previous years finally come true. Don't let the concerns of what is behind you stop you from pushing headlong into the life you've always wanted.

The 50 things contained in this book are not meant to be ironclad but rather serve guideposts to help you plan your future. You may commit to a few and reject others. Ultimately, by even implementing a few of them, you'll be much more prepared than you would be otherwise. At the very least, you need to have a plan, and that's how this book is meant to help you.

Ready to get started? I thought so! Let's get going.

1

TAKE UP A
SELFISH HOBBY

Assuming that you spent your life in any kind of traditional, nuclear family model, then chances are you spent most of your life being a responsible adult. There's nothing wrong with that; after all, somebody has to pay the bills, raise the children, and mow the lawn every once in a while.

But now is the time that you can afford to be a little selfish. Notice the key phrase there is "a little." You shouldn't go off the rails, but it's okay to indulge in some of the things you've always wanted to do if you had the time. Fishing, painting, drag racing — whatever it is, make sure that it's for you. Don't do it because you're trying to prepare for a project or because you want to make money off of it (although if that's what you want, see "Start a Business" below).

Ironically, the only way to be more self*less* in life is to be a little more self*fish*. It may seem counterintuitive, but a life that is spent endlessly saying yes to everything and everyone will leave little energy for you to later spend on the experiences, relationships, and causes that you really care about. You'll be much healthier, emotionally speaking, and will have a stronger sense of ownership of your life.

All of that being said, the whole point of this section is not to burden you with more responsibility. Instead, it's meant to give you the freedom to do whatever it is that you've really been wanting to do, regardless of all the "responsible" reasons you've had for saying no in the past. At this point in your life, you have the time and resources available to indulge your passion, so go for it!

2

INVEST IN THE HYPE

Have you ever played golf in Scotland? No? Okay, so you might not be the world's biggest golfer, but even if you're not, most of us have heard about the correlation between the history of golf and the famous courses at St. Andrews. It's almost a rite of passage for any serious golfer to play on the links at least once in their lifetime, even if it doesn't actually live up to the hype.

Perhaps, for you, it's not St. Andrews. Maybe, as a lover of ancient history, you're more into the pyramids. Or, to find something little closer to home, perhaps it's the silos at Magnolia for the *Fixer Upper* diehard in your life. Whatever your particular passion in life is, I guarantee that there is a place, event, or item that's associated with it that no serious student could ever really say that their life was complete without experiencing at least once.

So, visit the Taj Mahal, throw a coin in the Trevi Fountain, or spend a week at Everest base camp. If you've spent your whole life dreaming about what a place or experience must be like, go find out firsthand.

While there's always a chance that you could walk away feeling disappointed, there's also the very real possibility that it's greater than you ever imagined it to be in the first place. And when that happens—when you finally get to experience your dream—it's better than just about anything else on this earth.

3

GO REALLY, REALLY FAST

I still remember the day that I went joy riding as a 19-year-old in my friend's Corvette. We had a bit of pavement out in West Texas that stretched for a dozen or more miles at a time and was completely flat. My friend punched the accelerator, and we topped out at nearly 125 mph. Just for the thrill of it, I stuck my head out the window to see what it would feel like. I don't recommend that at all.

Speed limit laws aside, you owe it to yourself to go really, really fast at least once in your lifetime. There are plenty of perfectly legitimate ways to do this, like going to a speedway that offers Lamborghini or Maserati lessons. Sure, these may cost $300 to $500 a pop, and they may only last for about 15 minutes, but few things can compare to the feeling of going so fast that you're pushed back against your seat by the g-force. If you're fortunate enough to sit next to a trained race car driver to take you on this journey, it's even better.

If you want to go really, really, *really* fast, then you should see what life feels like in the back of a fighter jet. There are several places around the country that allow you to pay a couple of thousand dollars (no small amount of money, mind you) for a few hours in the back of a fighter jet. Your pilot will take you up, down, and side to side. They'll even do some barrel rolls and who knows what else to get you the full experience. I've never been on one of these, but it's on the list. I hear it's amazing.

4

EXAMINE YOUR SPIRITUALITY

There's something about driving at 125 mph that will force you to re-examine your spirituality and what you can expect when you die. You shouldn't wait until you're in a speeding Corvette to examine your spirituality. After you turn 50, it's worth considering what the next stage of your life will be, whether that's an afterlife or something else entirely.

Examine the great texts that ancient philosophers and spiritualists have compiled, such as the Bible, the Koran, and even the Veda, among others, to see how they compare. You'll probably notice a few similarities, but each one has its own unique take on what happens after you die, so it's a good idea to explore the differences between them.

Take care not to embark on this adventure with an air of skepticism. It's common for people who have never been religious before in their entire lives to simply skip over this chapter, but there are a lot of very practical reasons why you should take some time to investigate your own spirituality from an honest perspective.

For one, it may be that you've overlooked something important in your life; if so, then finding it now is better late than never. Secondly, doing so will help you gain some perspective on what your priorities should really be all about. The book of Ecclesiastes in the Bible, for instance, is written entirely from a nihilistic perspective; if nothing on this Earth can truly satisfy us, he argues, then what is life really all about? His answers are found in the pages that follow.

I talk about meditation, gratitude, and finding tranquility later in this book (see chapters 20, 24, and 27), but regardless, having a sense of spirituality will make you a deeper person, even if you never follow through on the texts themselves. Be sure to give them proper consideration as you may find some nuggets inside that will change your life for the better.

5

CREATE A
50-YEAR BUDGET

By the time you turn 50, you most likely have your financial endeavors well in hand. You probably have a mortgage or a car that is completely paid off. You've likely invested in a 401(k) or another retirement plan. Your Roth IRAs are most likely maturing, and your stock portfolios are looking nice. So, what is there to plan for, exactly?

Truth be told, if you're sitting in the above position, you're doing better than most. Most recent studies indicate that the average 50-year-old only has around $117,000 saved up for retirement. That number can fluctuate a little bit depending on the person's state and chosen occupation, but the reality is that most people simply have no understanding of what their spending will be like in the latter years of their life.

Many people mistakenly assume that when they retire, their average amount of spending will go down. After all, you don't have a lot of the everyday expenses that you had when you were younger, such as kids' activities, gas for your daily commute, or that expensive macchiato on your way to the office.

However, that doesn't mean that your expenses will necessarily go down. These can be easily replaced by breakfasts with friends at the local diner, more vacations, and expensive splurges. Many experts believe that you should anticipate your current spending level being at roughly where it is now, if not just a little bit more.

One thing is for sure: The absolute last thing you want to do when you get to this stage of your life is to rest on your laurels. You may have enough money in the bank to last until you're 70, but what about your quality of life when you're 80 and 90 years old? 100? Social Security and Medicare will pay for some of your expenses, but hospital stays, retirement homes, and increased expenses associated with living assistance will eat into your savings faster than you think. You should make a budget now so that you can realistically plot out your financial future until you're 100 years old. If you do that, you're all but guaranteed a comfortable retirement.

One of the best pieces of advice I've ever heard was from a lady who was 85 years old. She told me that she had worked when she was younger and saved for when she got older so that she could spend as much as she wanted to now. She told me that her goal was to live her life in such a way that she could do what she wanted, and the only thing that would bounce was the check to pay for her funeral. Her snarky laugh afterwards made me chuckle.

6

CREATE AN
ESTATE PLAN

If plotting out your budget until you are 100 years old scares you, then the idea of estate planning may be downright terrifying. But there doesn't have to be anything gloomy about planning for what to do with your assets once your life comes to an end; in fact, doing so may be one of the greatest gifts you can ever give your loved ones. Nobody, I repeat *nobody*, wants to deal with the headache of managing an estate when their loved one unexpectedly dies. Get it taken care of as soon as possible so that they can have peace of mind in the event that the unfortunate happens.

The good news is that this process is remarkably easy. Hopefully, when you were younger, you had an estate plan drawn up as to what would happen to your assets in the event that you and/or your partner passed away. If so, then all you need to do when you turn 50 is update it to reflect the changes that have happened since.

If you haven't done any form of estate planning, then it's not too late. Contact an attorney to help you track your last will and testament and designate someone to have power of attorney over your estate in the event you are incapacitated. You should also contact a fee-only financial advisor that can help you with your charitable giving to take advantage of certain tax strategies as you get older.

The other good news that comes with drafting an estate plan at this point your life is that you're most likely at the apex of your earning power. You should use this time in your life to your advantage to set up a schedule to pay down debts, invest more heavily in your portfolio, and draft other strategies that can set you up for the future. All these can be taken care of in less than a few weeks, so it's better to get started now.

7

PAY OFF DEBT

Despite what some people say, there is almost never a good time to have debt. Sure, it may be more financially sound to put your money into certain mutual funds that are growing at a faster rate when the interest rates on your debt are low, but the simple fact remains that debt can tie you down faster than just about anything else. More than one person has had to work well into their sixties, seventies, and even eighties to pay down the mortgage or other loans that should've been paid off well before then.

While your mortgage is the obvious behemoth in the room, there are other forms of debt that you should think about as well. Surprisingly, the fastest demographic of the general population that is accruing student loans are people in their fifties and sixties. They're either taking them out for their children, or they're taking them out to go back to school to further their own education. If that's the case, you should always pay them down as quickly as you possibly can in order to clear up that money for other expenses.

Other forms of debt that can be downright overwhelming are auto loans, personal loans, and credit cards. Although the interest on your car payment is most likely below 5% or 6%, credit cards and personal loans can have double-digit interest fees that can suck up an enormous amount of your monthly budget. The worst part is that none of those interest payments go towards the actual debt itself, which means you're not building any capital. Additionally, the more money that you have tied up in making monthly payments on debt, the less money you have to spend on other, more fun expenditures.

The name of the game when it comes to money after you turn 50 is flexibility and equity. The more flexibility you have to be able to pivot due to changing circumstances in life, and the more equity that you have to help buttress some of the situations, the happier and more stress-free your life will be. Plus, you'll most likely get to retire earlier than other people.

8

LEARN A LIFE SKILL

I don't know who you are personally, but I would be willing to guarantee that there is something in your life that you've always wanted to do, and yet have never found the time. Whether that's taking scuba diving lessons or learning how to play the guitar, there's an itch that you've always wanted to scratch without actually taking that next step.

Don't put it off any longer. If you've always wanted to start a band, then pick up an instrument and ask your buddies to come over for a jam session. With any luck, you'll also get some gigs at local hotspots. If you've always wanted to swim in the Great Barrier Reef but are terrified of snorkeling, then grab some cheap gear and head to your local pool to take the plunge first. Literally.

You are never too old to learn a life skill; in fact, doing so may help with the aging process. The reason that many people's cognitive functions decline as they get older is because they're not challenged enough. They refuse to stay active and challenge their mind and body, which results in mental and physical atrophy that makes it harder and harder for them to get out of bed. One of the best ways to keep that zeal for life and feel young even when you're knocking on the century mark is to constantly keep learning and growing.

One of the unexpected side benefits of this is that you'll most likely discover communities that you never even knew existed. Those who have spent their entire lives at their day jobs may be lost once they decide to finally retire and find that their only source of relationships was the people that they worked with in the office next door.

Learning a new skill immediately puts you in the company of other people who are not just there because they're getting paid to be, but rather because they genuinely *want* to be. Whether that's a bicycle-riding team, local authors' group, or even a competition barbecue team, learning new skill sets will immediately put you in the company of people with whom you have a lot in common.

9

TEACH A LIFE SKILL

At 50, you have a wealth of information at your fingertips. You've lived more life than most people in the history of humanity, and with the number of resources at your disposal in that time period, I'm sure you've also traveled and interacted with different people. Do you think you have a thing or two to share with others?

I do, and so do a bunch of others who will rely on your expertise to advance their own lives. Local community centers are always looking for educators who can teach night classes on a variety of different subjects, whether they're professional or recreational in nature. If you truly want to go the more professional route, consider becoming an adjunct professor at a community college or university nearby. The pay won't be very good, but the conversation and relationships that you form inside the classroom will be invaluable.

Don't believe me? Consider the story of Dale Carnegie, the famous motivational and efficiency guru whose books such as *How to Win Friends and Influence People* fundamentally changed the course of business development at the beginning of the 20th century. He got his start teaching night classes in New York City and slowly adapted the lessons he learned into his bestselling books.

If you don't think that other people have anything to learn from you, then head down to the local nursing home and start asking people about their own lives. Before long, you'll become spellbound by the stories and life lessons that just seem to pour from their mouths. You have those stories too, so the only thing you need to do is find an audience. In the age of the internet, when a YouTube channel or blog can be started in less than 10 minutes, there's no excuse not to share your knowledge with the world.

10

NEGOTIATE FOR A RAISE

When you're 25 and just starting out on your career, it's very common to be scared of your boss. Chances are that your boss is an industry veteran who has dealt with tons of whippersnappers exactly like you and has very little time to entertain your arguments for why you deserve more money. Right or wrong, that mentality is pervasive among many younger people.

When you're 50, the opposite is true. You most likely noticed that younger people are coming through the doors of your office building, armed with advanced degrees and internships at much more prestigious locations than yours. It may make you fearful that you'll be run out of your office sooner rather than later.

Instead of harboring that mentality and lying in wait for your "pink slip," examine your net worth and communicate it to your boss so that you're better able to increase your financial standing. After all, the one thing that you have that the fresh-faced newbie doesn't have is experience. You know exactly what it takes to get the job done, and you've dealt with a billion different scenarios that would have left most greenhorns white in the face. Use that knowledge to march into your boss's office and negotiate a raise.

As mentioned earlier, your fifties is when your earning potential is at its highest, so maximize that as much as you can in this decade by constantly angling for more, if possible. Don't be greedy and certainly don't be rude. However, don't be afraid to be a little bit more aggressive now than you were 20 years ago. You've earned it.

11

START A BUSINESS

One of the best things about the modern world is having access to all sorts of resources right at our fingertips — literally. YouTube channels, blogs, and online courses make it incredibly easy to learn a new skill and, just as importantly, how to leverage that skill into creating a business.

If you're the type of person who has always dreamed about taking charge of your own financial destiny and owning a business, then it's time to start. It doesn't really matter what size your business is or what you decide to sell. There's nothing like the experience of being your own boss. You can set your own hours, hire your own people, and pivot in whatever direction you feel is best. Whether you want to enter the traditional retail market or go online and challenge the likes of Amazon, the world is your oyster. Even better, there's nobody to report to and nobody watching over your shoulder to micromanage your day-to-day activities.

Unfortunately, that is also the one downside of entrepreneurship. Being your own boss means that you're responsible for your own failures; but listen to me carefully when I tell you that *one failure doesn't have to define you*. Many people are scared away completely by the prospect of being their own boss because they can't handle the pressure of making tough financial decisions. Rest assured that those types of decisions will become easier with time, and in the early goings, those types of financial decisions are probably much easier than the ones you're used to making—just for someone else's business.

Another reason people refuse to start their own business after they reach 50 is because they think that they're "too old" to be relevant. They conceptualize owning their own businesses in terms of decades, not years, which just isn't true. Ray Kroc was over 50 years old when he franchised McDonald's into the juggernaut that it is today, and Colonel Sanders was in his early sixties when he started KFC after a string of failures. There's literally no reason for you not to take the leap and start your own business.

Doing so will also help you financially prepare. If you're worried about retiring because you're afraid you won't have money in your latter years, then starting your own business is one of the best retirement plans you can have. By starting your business now, you could be completely hands-off in a matter of years, which means you'll reap the financial rewards of a growing business while not having to put as much time in yourself.

12

START A NON-PROFIT

If engaging in business isn't your type of thing, then consider starting a nonprofit instead. While the world could always use more businesses to deliver better products and services, we are also in dire need of nonprofits that contribute directly to a cause. Mothers Against Drunk Driving (MADD) and the Susan G. Komen Breast Cancer Foundation are just two examples of nonprofits that were started because their founders were directly impacted by a cause. Those foundations have gone on to do amazing work to make the world an overall better place.

We mentioned earlier that learning a new life skill could be one of your greatest emotional assets moving forward in life, and nothing rejuvenates the soul like working directly for a cause that you're passionate about. At this stage in your life, you have the financial resources and the flexibility—not to mention the wisdom and experience—to really make a difference in this world, so give careful thought to what you're most passionate about and attack it head on.

It should also be said that you can have both a thriving business and a dominant social cause as well. Many of today's businesses have a social wing that they contribute to directly. The shoe company Tom's, for instance, has a "Buy a Shoe, Give a Shoe" initiative where they donate a pair of shoes to a needy person every time somebody buys one. This type of philanthropic giving can go a long way in not only changing the world but also increasing your bottom line as well.

13

SCHEDULE ROUTINE CHECKUPS

Despite what you may think (and feel), your body will not fall apart once you turn 50 years old, but there are a number of health checks that your general practitioner will need to start implementing into your regular routine. The types of maladies that start to afflict people over the age of 50 will vary, but virtually everybody is at greater risk of joint issues, memory loss, obesity, vision problems, and cancer. Having regular checkups will help you spot these issues before they become major issues.

Some of the most common screening questions that you have with your regular checkups are ones that you should already be undergoing, such as blood pressure checks, blood work, and immunizations. Once you hit 50 years old though, you'll start to add screenings for colon cancer, skin checks, and an assessment for your joints. It may be hard to believe, but the average age for knee replacement surgeries are people between the ages of 45 and 65. Therefore, even if you don't feel like you need these checkups, it's smart to get them done.

If applicable, make sure you also add in screenings for cervical, breast, and prostate cancer. You may want to have a full hormone profile done or other additional testing to track fluctuations over time. These screenings are especially important if you have a family history of cancer or you fall into a certain high-risk demographic group.

The one positive to all of these checkups is that the survival rate for early diagnoses of many types of cancer is much higher than 20 years ago. Early detection is the key to a long life. These exams may be uncomfortable, but it's vital that you get them done regularly to ensure good health as you age.

14

LISTEN TO YOUR HEART (LITERALLY)

There's no magic line that suddenly appears when you're more at risk of heart disease than when you're not. However, statistically speaking, about one in every four deaths in America is due to heart disease. Someone in the United States has a heart attack roughly every 40 seconds.

Fortunately, a lot of research has proven that the earlier in life you get these issues under control, the better your long-term health will be. Heart health in your early forties is one of the greatest indicators of what kind of health you will have in your sixties and seventies, so now is the time to get your vitals checked. Have your doctor test your blood pressure, cholesterol, body mass index, and diabetes to see what changes you need to make in your diet and lifestyle. And if you're still smoking for whatever reason, stop it. Nothing will have a greater impact on your future health than putting the cigarettes down *today*.

In your forties, you might be tempted to put your health on the sideline as you raise your children and get your career lined up, but that's a surefire way to set yourself up for failure later in life. You don't need to go out and run a triathlon every weekend, but even adding 20 to 30 minutes of walking every single day, combined with a moderately improved diet (cutting out sugar or processed foods and adding more fruits and vegetables, etc.) will have a monumental impact on your life. Make those changes now before your doctor forces you to make the changes later.

15

LIMBER UP!

Stretching is oftentimes seen as the stepchild of weight training and cardio, but if you want to have improved quality of life after your 50th birthday, you shouldn't neglect it. Stretching daily will help keep your joints strong and improve your overall feelings of wellness. Make it a goal to stretch a few times a week, if not daily.

During exercise, focus on things that stretch your arms, back, neck, and hips. Bend over and try to touch your toes. If you're really aggressive, put your hands flat on the ground. Don't feel like you have to keep your knees straight; bending them slightly, especially in the early days, is not necessarily cheating. What you're shooting for with the stretch are balanced hips and strong hamstrings.

Stand up straight and rotate your hips side to side slowly, making sure that you turn a full 90°. Then, slowly swing your hips as if you're working a hula hoop. Keep your stomach in and your shoulders flat. Don't move too fast or else this exercise will become ineffective. Next, hold on to a nearby table and pull your ankle backwards to your hip. This will stretch your quads and improve your overall flexibility from the waist down.

Finally, give your arms a good stretch by putting your elbow next to your ear and stretching your arm backwards. This will help with your triceps, which are among the most important muscles in your arms. Bring your elbows down and pull your shoulders back, trying to hold your own hand behind your waist. Open up your chest, look straight ahead, and try to move your hands as far away from your tailbone as possible.

Once you are done with all these exercises, feel free to shake it out and do some active stretching (i.e., stretching while moving). All in all, this should only take you about 5 to 10 minutes and will pay off big time in the future when your friends are starting to slow down.

16

FOCUS ON YOUR DIET

If we're being honest, diet is the one thing that most of us hate to change more than anything else. Sure, we don't mind adding a few flexibility stretches and walking a mile or two every day. Switching foods, however, is almost heresy to some people, especially when it's so ingrained inside of your culture that it's nearly impossible to separate from who you are as a person.

Let me be the first to tell you that you don't need to change every single thing about your diet in order to make substantial improvements. The best changes are often those microscopic alterations that you make over time, such as substituting one type of salt for a healthier version or a low-fat version of the same. Many of your favorite dishes can be made much healthier and will taste almost exactly the same, so don't just write off this section as an impossibility.

Some of the things you want to do first and foremost are keeping your sodium levels down and your protein levels up. Both of these will help repair your muscles and joints after activity, which can break down your body faster as you get older. Try to ingest more calcium, only eat when you're hungry, and introduce more complex grains into your diet.

Also, if you've never tried your hand at cooking, now is an excellent time to start. You may find that you enjoy being in the kitchen so much that you want to pursue a second career! You'll also be able to craft meals to your liking and introduce items that you never would've thought about beforehand like fish and certain types of vegetables. You may be surprised not only by what kind of food you enjoy but also by how different types of foods can make you feel overall.

17

COMPETE IN A RACE

I get it... People who compete in races can be really annoying. They're always talking about their latest times, what venue they're going to that weekend, or which type of $400 shoes they're buying that will shave a few seconds off of their time. It's really kind of nauseating, isn't it?

But it's also invigorating. I used to be one of those people who absolutely hated races of any kind: marathons, 5ks, triathlons—you name it, I was against it. And then I tried a triathlon. I was blown away, not by the feeling of crossing the finish line, but by the camaraderie that happened along the way. Every part of my race, people were cheering me on, even the other competitors who were trying to beat me (allegedly). The people you compete alongside are really the best part of any race, precisely because you're all in it together and pushing each other to do your best.

That's why I believe everybody should try at least one race in their lifetime at some point. Whether that's your local neighborhood race or the professional-level

Ironman held in Kona, Hawaii, every year, it doesn't really matter. Entering some kind of competition will give you a serious energy boost.

Racing can also give you something to shoot for. It's easy to fall into a rut as we get older, and pushing yourself to constantly improve can be incredibly motivating. Moreover, you'll discover new areas around the world — and in your own backyard — that are absolutely stunning when you travel them on foot. Building a community around yourself is the cherry on top, but when you add all of these things together, you find out that it's not even about finishing the race — it's about competing in the first place. That sense of accomplishment can't be beat.

18

TRY OUT FOR A GAME SHOW

Who doesn't love game shows? Growing up, *Family Feud* was a constant in my household, and as I got older, it was replaced by shows like *Who Wants to Be a Millionaire* and *The Weakest Link*. When I was sick and laid up on a couch with a bowl of chicken noodle soup, nothing got me through the day better than Bob Barker and *The Price is Right*.

Game shows are a staple of Americana, and most of us have at least one show that we identify with on some level or one that we've always wanted to be on. If that's you, then I would strongly encourage you to try your best to get on a show at some point. It doesn't even really matter what show it is or if you win any money. The experience alone will be something you'll talk about for decades.

The process of actually getting on a game show is remarkably simple. It's just like casting for any other type of show that's on television except there are more of them. Since they need different people for every episode, they're always casting. Some of the harder trivia shows like *Jeopardy!* require an exam, and you'll usually be put on a waiting list to even be admitted into an audition pool. Some of the other ones may only require an application and a video audition, if that.

Even better, if you are selected to appear on a game show, you'll have to fly out to the location, most often in California. This affords you an excellent opportunity to take a family vacation that's built *around* your game show audition so that you and your family can make memories as well. And if you win, you come home with some awesome bragging rights. Few things look cooler on a mantle than a trophy from *The Voice*, for instance, so get out there and try to win!

19

TRY A NEW SPORT

Even if you don't fancy yourself an athlete, trying a new sport is a great way to make friends and get exercise that you may not otherwise. I understand that "exercise" is a relative term, since hurling a bowling ball down the lane isn't exactly the same as Michael Phelps doing the 400 m breaststroke, but at least you're more active than you would be on the couch watching Netflix. And hey, I've seen the PBA. Those guys generate a lot of sweat.

Generally speaking, there are two types of sports you can compete in: team or individual. Team sports will be harder since you'll need to find a league where you can compete. Still, if you can find a local softball or flag football team to join, do it. In some parts of the country, they even offer recreational full-fledged baseball, so people will do their best to make a 72-mph sinker drop completely off the table in front of you. Whatever your thing is, it's probably out there.

Individual sports are much easier and usually serve as the gateway for just about anybody to find an athletic passion. Golf is an all-time favorite, but don't discount activities that you can do with a partner, such as tennis or croquet. The cost barrier to enter some of these sports is remarkably low, and you can often find secondhand gear in online marketplaces or at local garage sales.

Finding a sport like this allows you to sink your teeth into something, get out of the house, and enjoy an activity that you can play for years to come. Who knows? Maybe you'll even find yourself on a professional circuit at some point. Stranger things have happened.

20

PRACTICE
SITTING STILL

Life is all about the go, go, go. We are constantly on the move, whether it's to work, kids' activities, school, or even just the grocery store. Our life is in a constant state of motion, and very few people ever take the time to sit down intentionally and think about it. Let's face it: when you are sitting down, you're either on your phone scrolling mindlessly through social media or you're asleep. Neither of those two activities are conducive to deep emotional and intellectual thought.

Even if you're not a person who enjoys meditation, I would encourage you to give it a try. There are lots of guides online for how to get into a truly deep state, but one of the simplest is to sit in a spot where it's quiet and dark and time your breaths with a stopwatch: two seconds of breathing in, two seconds of breathing out. You can change those lengths accordingly and find a style that works best for you.

The ultimate goal is to get into a state where you're truly clearing your mind. Focus on something that is transparent, emotionless, or still. Think of this as spring cleaning for your mind; by getting out all of these intrusive thoughts, you're clear to focus on what truly matters.

If meditation isn't your thing, then set aside some time for prayer. Talking to a higher deity is a great way to put your own life in perspective, and it helps to get some things off your chest that you may have a hard time dealing with otherwise. You also have the ability to talk through certain issues or ask for help as you move through them.

Whatever route you choose, make sure you spend some time every day sitting still. You don't need to be sitting cross-legged on the floor, but mute the TV and put your phone down. Allow yourself to be present with your thoughts for a few minutes of every day. You may not think that it matters that much, but I guarantee you, after a few days of contemplative thought, you'll recognize the benefits.

21

START WALKING

There is no shortage of research that proves just how effective daily walking can be for your mind, body, and soul. I know of one lady who has maintained a daily 20-minute walking habit from the time that she was 30 years old. When she was 65, she was in a bad car crash and broke her back in several places. Instead of being wheelchair-bound for the rest of her life, she was not only able to stand up straight inside of six months but also resumed almost all of her normal activities inside of a year. She credits that almost exclusively (besides fantastic medical care) to her daily walking habit.

Walking isn't a cure-all in and of itself; it's really the repetition of any kind of low-impact activity that does the trick. Even something as simple as swimming a few laps every single day, as long as it's consistent, will help your joints and your muscles stay active. Atrophy is one of the worst things that can happen to you as you start to get older, so make it a point to stay at least a little bit active every single day.

But walking does have certain benefits. It's a way to keep your legs active, get outside in nature, and experience the world around you. There's something different about walking through your neighborhood that makes it distinct from driving through it. You notice people's lawns, have conversations with other walkers, and get a strong breath of fresh air that fills your lungs. It's extremely therapeutic and you get some valuable time alone with your thoughts.

Best of all, walking is something that you can integrate alongside your current workout regimen. If you're the type of person who loves to hit the gym first thing in the morning, walking 20 to 30 minutes every day won't interfere with that. You can even start your workout with walking and end it the same way. It's low impact, aerobic, and a great way to ease in and out of any type of more strenuous activity.

22

DRESS HOW YOU WANT

I was an extremely self-conscious kid growing up. When I was in high school, the only thing I wanted to do was dress how I thought I *should* look, which included some of the worst combinations of pants and shirts known to man. Not only did it look awful, but it was also painfully obvious to everybody that I was trying too hard.

Unfortunately, some people never get out of that mindset, and truthfully, it took me a long time to get rid of it as well. One of the most liberating feelings you can have is owning your wardrobe. I don't mean owning it in the sense of "It's not on layaway anymore," but in owning it, as in, it's *your distinctive look*. It's your style, whatever that may mean to you, and you have no problem showing it off to the world because it represents who you are.

Now, before we get too far ahead of ourselves, I understand that certain offices and organizations have dress codes, and I am by no means insinuating that you should break those in some sort of teenage-esque rebellion phase. What I am suggesting, though, is modifying your wardrobe so that it reflects who you are. If you want to wear hot pink pants with flip flops, then by all means do so. For most people, adjusting their clothes might mean dressing more simply. It's about dressing how you want and wearing what makes you feel good instead of worrying about what's "in."

Even inside of the workplace, don't be afraid to let your true style shine. If the dress code in your office is business casual, then branch out and find some other ways that you can satisfy your personal tastes without being over the top. Explore what color combinations go well together, what types of pants go well with what shirts, and find the match that suits you best. And by all means, accessorize. Wear the pocket square, get the watch, try fancy socks — whatever it is you want to do. Experiment and watch the expressions on people's faces change as you walk into a room. Most likely, they won't even notice your brand-new threads — they'll notice your confidence.

23

ACCEPT YOUR FLAWS

We all have flaws. Nobody reading this right now is 100% perfect across the board. Either your hair is going gray, or you have a mole between your eyes that has always made you a little bit self-conscious. Or it may be something else entirely. Try as you might, it's virtually impossible to ignore something that you feel is a blemish.

I'm not asking you to forget that those exist; what I'm asking you to do is make peace with it. Very few people in this world have the means to change their appearance in any sort of significant way. Even if you do, finding the right doctors who will do that for you without making you look like you belong at Madame Tussauds wax museum is even more difficult. Rather than constantly springing for the next Botox injection or lip filler, learn to accept the things that make you who you are.

Think about Cindy Crawford. The supermodel who rocked newsstands through most of the 1990s has what she calls a "beauty mark" on her cheek. It's a mole just above her lip. She could've let that scare her away from modeling—and by all reports, many people in her early career *did* reject her for it—but it made her part of who she was. As a result, she not only became a superstar, but she also, somehow, became relatable.

That's ultimately what people want in relationships: somebody they can relate to. Your flaws—and more importantly, your acceptance of them—make you a human being, and other people will naturally let down their guard around you when they sense you won't judge. You'll be more confident, and the people around you will be more confident as well.

24

STOP COMPLAINING

Seriously, just stop it.

Nobody wants to hear it; nobody has anything to say back to it. If you're known as somebody who constantly complains about every single thing that happens in your life, nobody will want to be around you either. And guess what? That will give you one more thing to complain about.

Toddlers are great at complaining. They whine about lost Legos, food that's too hot or too cold, or the fact that they have to go to bed at a reasonable hour. But toddlers whining about those things is one thing; as an adult, you're expected to move past that. And yet, it never ceases to amaze me how many grown adults complain about some of the most trivial things. They get upset about their property taxes being too high or that their employer isn't matching dollar for dollar on their 401(k). Or something else just completely sets them off.

Are these things fixable? Absolutely. And if you want to do something about them, then by all means go ahead. But the last thing that you should do is walk around complaining about them to everybody who will listen while *refusing to actually take action*. If you're not happy about your property taxes, then file a complaint with a politician. I guarantee that the random stranger you met in the bread aisle at the supermarket doesn't care.

Instead, look for ways to be optimistic about things. As you turn 50, there's no doubt that one of the things that you are *less* optimistic about is your age. You may hear jokes about "being over the hill" or "not being a spring chicken," but look at those things as a source of pride. So many people throughout history have died well before their 50th birthdays, leaving them with a drastically shortened lifespan to try and experience all that life has to offer.

If you're in even moderately good health, you have essentially hit the genetic jackpot, and your 50th birthday should be a period of rejoicing. It should be viewed as a gift instead of some kind of curse that is happening to you. Look for ways to enjoy that gift and share joy with the people around you. Be the light in the world that you want to see—as cliché as it may sound—and put complaining to bed once and for all.

25

GO ON A TECH FAST

Technology is a wonderful thing, isn't it? It allows you to keep up with loved ones or manage your portfolio without having to pay expensive brokerage fees. It can connect you to far-off worlds and then help you find the best fares to reach them. All the while, the internet can broaden your horizons and allow you to engage with communities in ways that you never thought possible before.

It can also be an extreme time suck. We've all had the experience of scrolling through our social media feeds for what we thought was only a few minutes only to look up and see that an hour has passed us by. When you look back at that time, what do you have to show for it? Not much, I would gather.

For the sake of your own sanity, and the sanity of those around you, devote yourself to going on a tech fast. This can be either a few hours, a few days, or even longer, but commit to completely stripping yourself of all of the latest technology for a period of time. Even something as simple as committing to put your phone in a certain place for the entire day, only stopping to check for important messages a few times, can have a drastic impact on your health.

You'll become more present and probably less irritable to boot. We get angry because we feel like there are multiple demands on our time, but when 90% of the time is invested in technology, that leaves little room for other people and the more important things in life.

It can be hard to do it first, so take baby steps. Allow yourself to have the TV on but the computer off. Restrict your phone usage to a few minutes every day or turn on your phone's monitoring to alert you whenever you spend too much time on a certain app. Even implementing a few safeguards like this can help you be more aware of what kind of tech you are using so that you can better remove it when you know it's not necessary.

If you're like most people, you're probably so deep into technology that you don't realize just how much time you spend absorbing all of this information. It may be a shock to your system to not go to the same sites and scroll for hours and hours every single day, but it can also be one of most rejuvenating things you ever do.

Starting with a good book and a cup of coffee every morning instead of spending 20 minutes on your phone in bed can give you a more purposeful, relaxing beginning to your day. It can help make you more optimistic about yourself and less pessimistic about the world (especially if you start your day by reading the news). Embrace it.

26

MAKE A TRAVEL
TOP TEN

At the top of nearly everybody's bucket list is some sort of travel-related goal, whether that's to visit every country in Europe or spend a year living abroad. For some people, the allure of living in a foreign country — or even retiring in one — is almost too much to handle. Indeed, there are several advantages to living abroad as an ex-pat, such as cheaper healthcare, more affordable housing, and a better quality of life.

But assuming that your travel plans don't include living in a bungalow on a Mexican beach somewhere, chances are you still have a desire to visit other countries besides the one you were raised in. In fact, according to a recent poll, over two-thirds of people over 50 years old have "travel to another country" on their to-do list. Some of the most popular destinations include Paris, Tokyo, and Italy. But then again, those are on *most* people's bucket lists.

Instead of making it a goal to just visit one of these countries, I would encourage you to make a goal to visit 10 of them—namely, the 10 most interesting places to you. This allows for enough breathing room to not only hit the high points, like the ones that everybody else wants to visit, but also some off-the-beaten-path type places as well. For instance, while you most likely want to visit the aforementioned places, consider visiting Machu Picchu or taking a road trip through Portugal as well.

Give yourself the flexibility to change these destinations as you grow older. Making a goal to visit 10 of them will give you something to shoot for over a long period of time. Assuming that you visit one of these destinations every couple of years, this list should keep you busy for the coming decades. If you visit them all, you can always develop a new top 10 list.

As any traveler will tell you, though, simply visiting these countries usually isn't enough. If you do decide to spend some time in these areas, try to make it an extended trip of at least three weeks or more. This allows you to not only visit the more famous destinations, but also to really explore the country.

The south of France, for instance, is very different than Paris. By taking a few extra weeks and driving around inside its borders, you can truly appreciate the beauty that the country has to offer. Plus, you'll be able to immerse yourself in the true culture of an area. Try to learn a few words in the language before you go, and you'll be surprised how many people will be willing to help you along the way.

27

FIND YOUR OWN WALDEN POND

For bibliophiles, Walden Pond is synonymous with rest, relaxation, and meditation. Henry David Thoreau famously spent three years at the lakeside retreat of his close friend Ralph Waldo Emerson in the 19th century. As he sat by the pond, he wrote *Walden,* which is a treatise on simplistic living that's in harmony with nature itself.

That all sounds really awesome but finding a place that you can get away from it all isn't always as easy as it may sound. Even if you do secure your own version of Walden Pond, you often have to fight work schedules and heavy rush-hour traffic out of town. You might also face other logistical challenges getting yourself and all of your resources there. In fact, once you get there, it may seem like the exact *opposite* of harmony.

That doesn't mean you should give up on it. Walden doesn't have to be some far-off destination that requires a week of traveling; indeed, it can be found inside your own backyard — sometimes literally. More than one homeowner has converted their back yard into a veritable oasis, complete with fire pit, waterfalls, and lush greenery. There, in the sanctuary of their home, they find their escape.

As you grow older, it's more important than ever to find a place that you can truly call your own. As you begin to wrestle with some of the more complex metaphysical and spiritual realities of life, you may begin to realize that it's about more than just your career, your home, and even, in some cases, the relationships that you develop.

Thoreau's greatest revelation during his time at Walden Pond was not that he had spent his life pursuing meaningless activities, but they had lived his life without any purpose at all: "I went to the woods because I wished to live deliberately, to confront only the essential facts of life, and see if I cannot learn what it had to teach, and not, when I came to die, discover that I had not lived."

These words are a sobering reminder of the sanctity of life and how we must live every single day with intentionality. Going after the big things and tackling huge questions enriches our lives and gives them purpose. Don't be afraid to find your own version of Walden Pond. When you do, spend as much time as necessary to gain a deeper understanding of your own life.

28

TAKE UP READING

When Bill Gates was still the CEO of Microsoft, he would leave headquarters twice a year for about a week each time and take a stack of documents up to a remote cabin in the middle of Oregon. He'd do nothing but read from sunup to sundown. Sometimes, he took a book along with him, but that was only if he was feeling adventurous; his main diet consisted of industry reports, project proposals, and other materials that Microsoft employees had sent to him to consider.

Even though he's not technically the head of Microsoft anymore, Bill Gates still spends quite a bit of time in seclusion reading—about an hour a day on average. He, along with other billionaires like Elon Musk and Warren Buffett, credit the monumental amount of reading that they do every day to their success. It allows them to open up entire worlds that were previously uncharted, exploring other universes and interacting with thinkers from all across history in an effort to expand their own minds.

Reading is one of the best ways that we constantly grow, not only intellectually but emotionally as well. It doesn't matter if you prefer fiction or nonfiction. The simple act of picking up a book (or a Kindle, if you're so inclined) signals a desire to actively learn rather than to be passively entertained. Mental stimulation is the most obvious benefit of a daily reading habit, but so is improved vocabulary and sharper analytical skills as well as reduced stress. Habitual readers are a lot like fitness enthusiasts in that way — they can't imagine their lives without it because it makes every other aspect so much better.

C. S. Lewis famously said, "In reading great literature I become a thousand men and yet remain myself. Like the night sky in the Greek poem, I see with a myriad eyes, but it is still I who see. Here, as in worship, in love, in moral action, and in knowing, I transcend myself; and am never more myself than what I do." For those who are over 50 and terrified about not squeezing as much out of life as possible, reading provides a mental escape that allows you to live 100 lives at the same time without ever having to leave your armchair.

29

COMMIT YOURSELF
TO HONESTY

Why do we lie? Some experts would argue that it is out of a sense of self-preservation, while others are just simply entertained by it. Regardless of the reasons, it's easy to argue that in every form of dishonesty, there is at least a hint of insecurity. Whether you can't face reality, or you're afraid that other people can't, deceitfulness is a shortcut to avoiding some of the most painful truths of life.

At the age of 50, there's no need for that anymore. You're secure with who you are, and you've done a lot of great things and made a lot of great friendships along the way. It's time to have little confidence in yourself. While I'm not accusing anybody who is reading this of being an outright liar (far from it, in fact), there are little marks of deception that can appear in everyday life: stories we tell, taxes we file, daily conversations with our coworkers, etc. Embellishment is one thing, but intentional deception is quite another, and at this stage of your life, it's time to commit yourself to being 100% honest whenever possible.

And lest you think that this is some sort of an excuse to be rude, think again. A lot of people will complain about the food at their local restaurant, for example, under the guise of them simply wanting to "be honest." You can still be honest about things without indulging some kind of weird desire to be mean. The last thing you want to do is grow more antagonistic as time goes on, so work on always telling the truth, but doing so *in love*.

Over time, you'll find that a life lived honestly — and one that is lived honestly towards *other* people — is a very freeing and fulfilling life. You allow yourself to be real, not only with yourself but also with those around you. It's authentic, and you may even find that it sharpens your skills of perception to be able to pick up on little cues here and there. It's important to be self-aware as you age, but that's only if you've committed yourself to being honest with the results in the process.

30

DEVELOP DEEP RELATIONSHIPS

I'll never forget the day that my father finally retired from his career. After a string of somewhat successful jobs up to that point, he had finally found steady employment at a factory where he stayed for over 30 years, eventually rising to the ranks of upper management. I was proud of him, but more importantly, he was proud of himself. He had earned this retirement and was looking forward to leaving gracefully.

But on his last day of work, he showed up at home sooner than we had all anticipated. My mother asked him why he was home so early, and with somewhat hurt eyes, he told her that his retirement party had simply ended sooner than he'd thought it would. It was only later — several years down the road, in fact — that I learned the painful truth: Very few people had actually showed up to congratulate him and say goodbye.

My father wasn't always the friendliest human being in the world, but he was far from the gruffest. As I've grown older, I've realized that his story is far more common than we realize. The people that we surround ourselves with at work, where we spend the vast majority of our adult lives, are not usually there to make friends. They're there to make money and to advance their own careers (nothing wrong with that, by the way). If relationships happen as a byproduct, then so be it. There are always exceptions to this rule, of course; after all, I'm sure that you have close friends where you work. But don't be surprised if, as time goes on, those relationships don't always go as deep as you would have expected.

That's why it's important to develop deep relationships, intentionally, with people that you *truly* care about. Even people that you already have relationships with, such as your family and friends, can still benefit from focused attention. Take an interest in what they're going through and explore other hobbies that you may not have considered. Don't be afraid to stay up late into the night having long, meaningful conversations about real questions. Those are the times when you're going to find out the most about these people, so start that process as soon as you can.

31

FACE YOUR STRONGEST FEAR

"Do one thing every day that scares you."

It's hard to know who to attribute this quote to since variations of it have been associated with everyone from Ralph Waldo Emerson to Eleanor Roosevelt. The sentiment remains the same regardless: Live every day a little dangerously. Discover your fears and attack them head on, because in doing so, you will grow exponentially and usually in different ways than you expect.

The natural, *human* thing is, of course, to retreat from our fears as much as possible. If you're afraid of heights, you may choose to only work on the first couple floors of an office building, which may limit your career path. If you're squeamish about fast food, then maybe you've taken a career as a chef so that you can learn how to prepare your own and avoid the "unknown" part of food prep.

Regardless, the path that you've chosen so far in your life is at least partially attributed to what you want to avoid as much as what you actually want to do. While that's not necessarily a bad thing, it can preclude you from certain opportunities. A fear of flying, for example, means that you'll most likely never be able to travel the world, at least with any efficiency.

Of course, some of this might need to be scaled back. A fear of wrestling an alligator isn't really a fear *per se* as much as it's just a natural warning sign of danger. There's no practical reason to face that fear. But if you have even the slightest inkling that your emotional objections have kept you back from living a full life, then now's the time to jump in with both feet and face them. I've heard of one person who had a fear of open water, and now she's a professional wakeboarder. Go figure.

In most cases, it's not about the fear itself as much as it is about gaining the willpower to overcome it. While this may not be important to you now, it will undoubtedly become more urgent of an issue as your life goes on. When we look back on our lives, we'll all acknowledge certain regrets no matter how fearlessly we've lived our lives. But undoubtedly, some of those regrets will be ones that are completely avoidable if you take action now. Even if you don't end up enjoying the thing that you're afraid of, you'll still take pride in the fact that you didn't let an emotional response stop you from trying, and that's reason enough to face your fears head on.

32

WRITE A BOOK

It's been said that everybody, no matter who they are, has at least one book inside of them. That might be a nonfiction book or a fiction story about aliens invading an underground tunnel beneath San Francisco. No matter how far off or wild the proposition might sound, I'm a firm believer in this position as well: No matter who you are or what stage of life you're in, you have a story to tell. Tell it. "But I don't know how to write a book! I'm not a creative person, and I'm not enough of an 'expert' on anything to even write 1,000 words, much less 60,000!"

Nonsense. If you've lived longer than ten minutes, you're an expert on *something*. At the very least, you have a passion that is worth investigating and then writing about. As for the argument that you're not creative enough to tell a story? I would argue that you just haven't tapped into that side of your personality yet.

There's no doubt that some people are better at telling stories than others; I'm under no illusion that my writing is on par with Stephen King's, for example. But

I also believe that storytelling goes back to some of our most primal roots as human beings. A long time ago, when man was first starting to learn how to survive on this earth, they had to pass down bits of information about what to avoid, what to eat, and where to live. As time went on, stories about their own history or what they'd seen in their travels started to be transmitted from person to person, resulting in—you guessed it—storytelling. Whether the goal was to inform or to entertain, we relied primarily on an oral-based culture.

The dual nature of fiction and nonfiction accomplishes both of those goals. If you don't have a creative bone in your body, chances are you're working in some kind of technical field. If that's the case, then maybe a nonfiction book is for you. If you spend most of your lunch hour dabbling with cartoons or attempting to write responses to prompts that you find online, then fiction is probably your jam.

One of the reasons I'm so passionate about writing stories is that I believe it unlocks the creative force that exists in all of us. You can use this creative force to excel at your current job, allowing you to think outside the box to tackle complex problems that you may face on a daily basis. It will also make for livelier dinnertime conversation as you relate your day in a way that is engaging to those around you. Increasing your own creativity can help in a myriad of different ways, even if you never actually "finish" your book.

Writing a book is a very labor-intensive operation. For some, this may take a few months while others will spend upwards of a decade writing a story. There's even a month dedicated to this. NaNoWriMo, which stands for National Novel Writing Month, is celebrated by authors every November. I would encourage you to take the challenge and see what you produce at the end of that month.

And if you feel the need to publish it, you don't have to sit around and wait for Simon & Schuster to come knocking on your door. These days, you can publish it yourself on sites like Amazon and Barnes & Noble and even earn a residual income off of it. There are several indie authors today who are making respectable salaries writing and publishing stories. Who knows? You might be the next one.

33

SIT IN THE FRONT ROW

If given the choice, I always prefer live events to watching them on TV or online (which, I would imagine, is the same for most people). Unfortunately, doing so can be quite expensive. When *Hamilton* was blazing up the stage all over North America, I knew I had to buy tickets for my wife and me to experience the phenomenon firsthand, even if that meant shelling out $350 for nosebleed seats. From where we sat, the only thing I could see was a bunch of tiny dots dancing around on stage.

I'm trying to become a more reasonable person about spending that kind of money on in-person events, but it's difficult. There's something about being in the "room where it happened" that just makes you feel connected to what's occurring onstage. With how ticket prices can get these days though, it's harder and harder to make that a reality.

Regardless of cost, I would challenge you to, at least once, shell out the big money to sit up close within a dozen or so rows from the stage. You may be forgiven for thinking that it's the exact same show that you've always seen, but I guarantee that you'll notice different nuances and expressions that you've never seen before. And, since a live event changes a little bit every time it's performed, you may even see something that nobody has ever seen before. I guarantee you the people in the back won't have a clue.

Honestly, it's like having your own private performance put on by some of the biggest mega stars of the day. They may not be performing for only you, but when very few people are in your periphery, it feels much more intimate than it would be otherwise. To get *that* experience—an actual private performance—would cost tens of thousands of dollars, if not more. When you put it in that perspective, paying for front-row seats is a real bargain, isn't it? At least that's how I explained it to my wife. She didn't really buy it, either, but we both enjoyed the experience, nonetheless. I can bet that you will too.

34

WRITE LETTERS

Many experts believe that we are living in one of the most information-rich times in history. Between the internet, social media, and email, the world is currently in the middle of an explosion of documentation, where people are updating the rest of the world on what they had for dinner, where they're going on vacation, and what their political beliefs are. What a time to be alive.

Unfortunately, the reality is that unless these thoughts are written down, there's very little chance that they'll actually survive any distance into the future. All it takes for years and years of pictures and memories to go down the drain is for Facebook's servers to suddenly explode. More likely, they'll just suffer a catastrophic power failure that compromises an essential storage function. Seriously, the only thing that separates us from years of lost pictures is someone flipping the wrong switch. If that happens, you'll notice collective shock from billions of people who rely on it to keep track of their lives.

By contrast, letter writing establishes a much more permanent record of your day-to-day operations. When you write letters to family members or friends, it's a much more personal touch that they'll appreciate, especially in a day and time where almost everything we pull out of our mailbox is a bill or a notice to extend our car's factory warranty. *No, thank you!*

Plus, chances are, unless the recipient has a severe lack of space in their house, they'll most likely keep that letter. They can read it later whenever they want to. Moreover, they may decide to read it 10 years down the line. Then, 100 years later, when their descendants are going through their belongings, they may read it again and gain an understanding of what life was like when you were alive. Realistically speaking, it may be that historians, centuries from now, rely on your writings to recreate everyday life, which would make you a future celebrity. It could happen!

But even if nobody else ever reads your letters besides you and your recipient, it's still a good practice to get into. Studies have shown that writing down our thoughts helps us navigate complex ideas more effectively. Before juggling a difficult decision, writing a letter to a loved one allows us to voice those thoughts and see them more clearly. It also helps you get your emotions out on paper rather than internalizing them.

People who write by hand regularly report less pent-up anger and sadness than those who choose to bottle their feelings up. Writing letters most likely won't save your life, but it can't hurt either.

35

WORK ON YOUR GENEALOGY

It seems like every family has at least one member who is absolutely obsessed with genealogy. They're always wanting to show you the latest family pictures that they found or cemetery listings of people that you've never heard of (but absolutely should have, obviously).

It can be tempting to simply smile and nod at these people, but the next time they start talking to you about distant ancestors, pay attention. While you may not recognize names, putting these people together in your mind may uncover a treasure trove of information about where you came from, as well as give you a deeper understanding of your own personal history.

It's always exciting to learn about a distant family member who fought in a famous battle or did something semi-important in history. What's also exciting is realizing that you are distantly related to a celebrity. Remember several years ago when someone discovered that Brad Pitt is Barack Obama's fifth cousin? What a weird connection! But also extremely interesting.

Besides the obvious benefits of making connections to people throughout history, you may also learn information that's relevant to who you are as a person. For instance, uncovering a long line of family health issues can help keep you aware of the things you need to look for as you get older. Are most of the people in your family dying before the age of 80? It might be worth the trip to your doctor to discover why.

On a less gloomy note, though, you may also find out that you're entitled to land or property that you didn't know about otherwise. In fact, somebody out there right now may be searching for your specific family just so they can return something of value to you; even if it's not financially advantageous, it may still be meaningful. Regardless of your reason for investing in your genealogical roots, you can be guaranteed that doing so will be an intriguing study as you learn more about where you came from and the different individuals who make up your ancestral history.

36

WALK THE D-DAY BEACH AT NORMANDY

If you've never been to the beaches of Normandy, it's an incredibly sobering experience right up there with visiting the Arlington National Cemetery and the battlefield at Gettysburg. Occupying a very distinct moment in history—not just American, but global—the northern beaches of France are a generational landmark that exemplifies what it means to be both courageous and patriotic.

Although some people have issues with certain monuments and territories because of what they represent, virtually everyone is in agreement that the soldiers who stormed the beaches of Normandy were some of the bravest people that our world has ever produced. Many of them were kids; the average age of soldiers during Operation Overlord was 20 years old. That includes officers as well as the soldiers who ran onto the beach. Many of the soldiers were much younger than that, with some having barely reached their 16th birthdays.

The people who ran onto the beach were as diverse as they come. Soldiers, officers, chaplains, medics, photographers, and even well-known figures were among them. President Theodore Roosevelt's son, Theodore Roosevelt, Jr., was a Brigadier General who ran onto shore with his men in the first wave at Utah beach. Even though he would die from health issues shortly afterwards, he is credited with helping organize trucks, men, and supplies on the beach to get them away from danger. When asked about the single most heroic action he had ever seen in combat, General Omar Bradley didn't hesitate: "Ted Roosevelt on Utah Beach."

As you walk the beach, try to imagine what those people went through in comparison to your own life. These men paid the ultimate sacrifice when they were a fraction of your age. Many never married, never saw their own kids, and would never see the end of the war.

And yet here you are, about to turn 50 years old—an age that most of them wouldn't see. It can feel like time is slowly slipping away, but what it should do is remind us how grateful we are to be alive. We've seen things and experienced much more of life than those men ever will. Yet the only reason we're able to have these moments is because of their sacrifice. It's a sobering reminder to be thankful for every second that we have on this Earth and to make the most of every opportunity we're given in the future.

37

TRY SURPRISE CHARITY

The first time I was ever in a "pay it forward" line, it was at a Starbucks near my house. I had no idea what was happening when I pulled to the front of the line and the person there informed me that the people in front of me had paid for my drink, and that—if I wanted to—I could pay for the drinks for the car behind me as well. Confused and surprised, I obliged, even though their $14 order was way more than my $3 drip coffee. Still, it somehow felt worth it.

Surprise charity is not a recent thing, but it's had a resurgence of sorts thanks to social media. Every once in a while, a news article will pop up showing an event like this in action or one that has recently finished. A Dairy Queen in Minnesota, for instance, racked up nearly $10,000 in sales when 900 cars "paid it forward" for the cars behind them. Customers were in tears as they thought about the generosity of other humans and were more than happy to keep the chain going for nearly two whole days.

Isn't that amazing? Granted, there is nothing special about getting a $3 ice cream cone for free, but it's the fact that somebody else was thinking enough of you to pay for it without any expectation of what they might receive in return. Chances are, if you've been a part of one of these lines, you won't ever forget it. Generosity breeds generosity, and while there's no guarantee that any generosity you show will be repaid by others, it doesn't really matter. After all, as they say, it's the thought that counts.

So, what can you do to pay it forward? Start with something small like picking up the tab of somebody in a restaurant regardless of whether you feel like they necessarily "need it." Become a "secret Santa" for the holidays and leave gift cards for nearby restaurants on the doorsteps of newlyweds or young parents. Head over to GoFundMe.com and find a few charities that you can support even if you've never heard of them. These may seem like tiny things, but as the combination of all of us pulling together makes a difference. Even if nobody else follows you in a surprise charity train, at least you've done your part.

38

GET LIFE INSURANCE

Do you know that only 54% of American adults actually have life insurance? It's a staggering figure and one that can be explained by a person's relative expectation of mortality. Since younger people naturally feel like they won't die anytime soon, they're not inclined to buy it, which can skew the numbers. But whether you feel like you need it or not, life insurance is one of those things that can save your bacon—or more specifically, that of your family—if something suddenly happens to you.

Most experts recommend that you should get around 10 to 15 times your annual household income when you buy life insurance. If your yearly salary is $60,000, for example, try to find a policy that gives you anywhere between $600,000 and $1 million. That may seem like a lot of money, but when you factor in the cost of paying off the everyday bills, long-term debt, and having something to get your loved ones back on their feet until their situation becomes more stable, it can vanish in a hurry. After all, the last thing that you want them to worry about in the wake of an untimely death is getting past-due notices on the mortgage.

The good news is that just about all life insurance is affordable and extremely convenient to apply for even at 50 years old. Though you'll probably need to have a physical (in some cases, you can use your regular annual physical instead) which saves you an extra out-of-pocket expense. Moreover, a life insurance application may alert you to various health issues that you can change to statistically increase your life expectancy like quitting smoking or improving your cholesterol numbers.

How much you decide to spend on life insurance depends both on your age and how much coverage you want on your policy. A 50-year-old who wants $250,000 of coverage, for example, can expect to spend around $50 a month. That same 50-year-old should expect to spend three times that much, or around $175, for $1 million. As with everything else, it's important to shop around in order to get the best rates, but once you find a policy that you think is adequate, sign up sooner rather than later. It's quick, easy, and extremely important.

39

SEE THE NORTHERN LIGHTS

There are few things in this world that truly take our breath away. The birth of a child, the sight of Victoria Falls in Africa, and skydiving could be a few. An opportunity that should be high up on your bucket list, no matter what else is there, is seeing the northern lights. Technically called aurora borealis, the northern lights are described as a "magnetosphere disturbance that is caused by solar wind" and produces a natural light display during the nighttime hours.

But that scientific description doesn't really do the experience justice. It's more accurately described as nature's light show, one that is equal parts unpredictable and awe inspiring. Hundreds of years ago, the northern lights were seen as harbingers of war or famine while others simply believed that they were reflections of campfires and torches in the night sky. People may have described the phenomenon in different ways, but those who are fortunate enough to see it claim that it's an experience that is unlike any other on earth.

The best places in the world to see it are located along the Arctic Circle in places such as Alaska, Canada, Iceland, Norway, and Finland. You'll want to go at night, but if you can, try to catch them through December and March. Some have even seen the northern lights appear as early as August. As there is more night during this time period, there's a greater chance of seeing the lights. It's also possible to see the southern lights, or aurora australis. As rare as the northern lights are, the southern lights are exponentially more difficult to see.

It can be hard to time a trip to see the northern lights, but if you're fortunate enough to catch them, it's a moment that you will treasure forever. Even those who live in the Arctic Circle still stop and take it all in whenever they see them appear in the night sky. Visiting nature of any kind is always impressive but seeing the wonders of the universe displayed in our nighttime sky can make us feel more connected to the divine as we tap into something that is larger than ourselves.

40

TRY COMMUNITY THEATER

For those who are unfamiliar or inexperienced with community theater, the name says it all: it's community. All (or nearly all) of the participants are somewhat local, and it's theater, which means it's an artistic endeavor. Most communities of any size have one, although you may have to search a while to find auditions and events near you.

Many people are scared away by community theater primarily because they have a very real fear of getting on stage. At this part of your life, chances are that you've at least worked through some of that. If not, community theater is a great way for you to open up. After all, it's much easier to get up on stage in front of other people when it's somebody else's lines and everybody else is telling you what to do.

I've tried community theater a few times and it's absolutely a blast in every way. Not only is it a great way to spend a Tuesday night, but it's also an amazing opportunity to meet people in your area. I've made lifelong friends through community theater simply by sharing a stage and performing in a somewhat decent version of *Fiddler on the Roof.*

Just as important though, it gives you a sense of pride. Although you won't win an Oscar for your performance — contrary to the opinions of some people you will undoubtedly share the stage with — you will get to perform in front of friends and family members who will probably come out in droves to support you. That final bow before the curtain falls as you stand next to your fellow castmates is a feeling that cannot be replicated, especially if you've never done anything like it before.

And don't feel like it has to be a permanent commitment either; just like regular theater houses, community theaters operate in seasons. You might do one play in the fall and another one in the spring. It's also not a lock that you'll get a role in either. Just like in other theaters, you'll have to audition for parts. Prior experience obviously does help. If you try it once and find that you don't like it, then move on to something else. At the very least, you'll still have those weeks to think back on and most likely remember quite fondly.

41

SPEND WAY TOO MUCH MONEY ON SOMETHING

When you're young, adults usually tell you to watch your pennies. We invest wisely, make sure that our bills are paid, and set up a savings account so that we know we have enough money to retire on.

But every once in a while, something really shiny comes along that catches our eye. We can't stop thinking about it. It might be a new car or a boat. It could just be a really expensive watch. At least once in your life, no matter how much it costs, *buy it.* Embrace that little devil that sits on your shoulder telling you to go for it.

Now, please hear what I'm *not* telling you. I'm not saying to take out a second mortgage on your house and spend frivolously on an item that you know you won't love or use. It makes no sense to buy something that will send you spiraling into bankruptcy. As long as you know your own means, you should be able to determine the difference between splurging and going overboard. Buying a private island, for instance, is usually way too expensive (unless your name is Richard Branson), but a couple acres out of the country that you can go hunting on? That's not nearly as big of a deal.

It's all about scale. What seems exorbitant to me may not be for you. When you buy this luxury item, especially if you've had your eye on it for a long time, you'll most likely treasure it forever. Look at it as a reward for all the hard work you've done in your career to get to this point. It's a celebration. Enjoy it.

If you've been putting off a large purchase for any length of time simply because that little voice in your head tells you that it's unnecessary, I would encourage you to shut out the doubt at least once. You can return it if you truly don't feel like it's right for you, but you deserve to be a little unreasonable every once in a while.

42

INVEST IN PICTURES

Just as we talked about with letter writing, one of the biggest issues of the digital age is that almost everything is electronic. We snap pictures that may or may not saved to our hard drive. As soon as we press the capture button, they're out of our memories forever. Snapchat and Instagram stories are gone even quicker, and there's virtually no record of what the moment looked like outside of what's in your own memory.

You may not realize it now, but pictures are going to be more important to you as time goes on. Your memory won't be as sharp as it is now at some point in the (very) distant future. Those things you can recall with ease now will be harder to remember later, if not forever. A picture captures those moments, allowing you to remember those precious moments and recall the context.

The best part about this is that taking pictures has never been easier. Your parents most likely had to spend quite a bit of cash for a roll of film and make each one of them count in order to get a good picture. In addition, they didn't even know what they had until the pictures were developed. These days, you can take hundreds of pictures per minute and examine each one of them to make sure the angle is perfect. Moreover, with different attachments for your smartphone, you can take some really professional-looking shots from a distance, up close, and with various depth-of-field alignments, if so inclined.

If you're the type of person who already has a whole bunch of photos, consider organizing them into months and years or even sorting by special moments and themes. A variety of different online services will send you pictures every month inside a mini-book, which make for perfect mementos to put on your shelf and pull down later. If you have a whole bunch of pictures that are older and sitting in a shoebox somewhere, take some time to organize them in a scrapbook. Traveling down memory lane is a fun trip but be sure you have the photos to make it possible.

43

TAKE CARE OF
YOUR TEETH

Just about everybody worries about something when they get older, like their bones not being as strong or their back suddenly hurting. But one thing that nearly everybody stresses about to a certain extent is their teeth falling out. Unfortunately, for people over 50, there's no tooth fairy to come along later, slipping a free baseball ticket or $100 bill underneath your pillow. Since there's no financial advantage to losing your teeth — and no other teeth coming in to replace them — you should prioritize them moving forward.

You know the typical cleaning procedures: brush twice a day, floss, use mouthwash, and get periodic checkups. But one area that you might not have thought of before is your gums. Red and inflamed gums are usually a sign of bacterial infection. While that might be annoying by itself, scientists have also found links between gum disease and heart issues. Excessive plaque buildup can eventually travel down your digestive track and get absorbed into the bloodstream, which can cause blockages if enough is accumulated. While cleaning your teeth regularly obviously won't necessarily negate a bad diet, there's no doubt that poor teeth cleaning can negatively impact your overall health.

The silver lining in all of this is that dental technology has advanced to such an extent that very few people need to worry about losing their teeth until they're much, much older. Even people in their nineties can have a full set of pearly whites as long as they get regular checkups and take care of their teeth. As the saying goes, an ounce of prevention is worth a pound of cure, so the earlier you take care of your oral health, the better chance you have of retaining strong teeth and gums well into your later years.

44

CUT BACK ON ALCOHOL

One of the main rules of aging is that you can't expect to maintain the same type of habits (at least with the same intensity) that you did when you were younger. That includes your drinking habits. While a glass of red wine has been proven to actually improve your cardiovascular health, drinking massive amounts of beer and hard liquor can wreak an exponential amount of damage on your body.

There's less water in your body as you get older, which means that there is also less water to flush out the alcohol in your system. Alcohol stays inside your liver longer, which can damage the liver quicker. It also doesn't allow your body to filter out other contaminants as well, which can cause *more* health issues. You might also notice a larger waistline. That added weight puts strain on your body and can cause your bones to deteriorate faster. And, since your immune system can be compromised by alcohol consumption, certain types of cancer have an easier time growing as well.

As you would expect, your tolerance for alcohol will go down after you turn 50. That means you'll get drunk faster and will experience harsher hangovers with longer periods of inebriation. If you're taking medications, alcohol can actually *reduce* the effectiveness of some of them while simultaneously accelerating the rate of others like aspirin and sleeping pills. Finally, those who have a problem with alcohol later in life report other issues, such as poor balance, poor reaction time, diabetes, high blood pressure, dementia, and impaired sexual function. As you can tell, reducing your alcohol intake as you age helps in at least a dozen different ways.

Everybody is different, but 50 years old is a great time for you take a close look at your health and honestly assess whether your alcohol habit could lead to more severe issues down the road. If so, dial it back a bit.

45

CHECK YOURSELF MORE OFTEN

Health is always something that you should value at any stage of your life, and routine checks should be implemented alongside your regular physicals and yearly checkups. However, you shouldn't rely on those to catch everything; indeed, a lot of issues can be detected at home. These days, even something like an at-home colon check can be performed (which is not nearly as bad as it sounds).

In addition, you should constantly be checking your body for any unusual moles or skin tags that seem to appear out of nowhere. Usually, the skin is the best place to identify early signs of something happening underneath it within the body. So, if anything looks off, have it checked by a dermatologist. You can also monitor your blood pressure and your vision at home; if those are reading outside of your normal bounds, schedule a checkup. Finally, have your bloodwork done at least once a year to determine if anything unseen could be forthcoming.

Outside of the regular health assessments, there are a number of different fitness tests that you can take to see how your endurance and cardiovascular system stack up. One of the best ways to check your overall health is to walk up four flights of stairs; if you can do that in under a minute, experts claim, you're in above average health. Another simple test involves stepping onto and off of a 12-inch-high stair for three minutes at a comfortable pace. Check your pulse at the end of those three minutes; if it's above 125 beats per minute, that's a good indication that you need to work on your aerobic activity.

Strength, balance, and flexibility are three other areas that you should check semi-regularly. For strength, you should be able to do at least 30 sit ups in under a minute, and for balance, you should be able to stand on 1 foot for at least 30 seconds. Your time will go down as you get older, so check it fairly often and work on your overall fitness to improve your times.

46

START A SKINCARE ROUTINE

There's no way to turn back the hands of time but having a solid skincare routine is the closest thing to it. You can look younger by establishing a good routine of simple over-the-counter skincare products on a daily basis. Try to avoid harsh masks and exfoliates since they can wreak havoc on your skin. Lotions that contain alcohol can also dry you out. If at all possible, avoid excessive sun, wind, and cold exposure, too.

Lest you think that this is all about vanity, you should know that hormones begin to change quite a bit after the age of 50. Estrogen isn't produced at the same rate due to menopause, which is responsible for trapping in moisture and encouraging collagen growth. This can cause your skin to thin and create wrinkles, which weakens the barrier between the environment and the inside of your body. In addition, healthy skin also encourages new blood vessel formation and rapid cell growth, not to mention the fact that taking care of your skin just makes you feel better. Most of us know what it feels like to have dry and cracked skin, and it's not the best feeling in the world.

For best results, use a facial cleanser in the morning and apply a serum that promotes skin growth. Moisturize after that and finish your skincare routine with a layer of sunscreen. All in all, your whole routine should take you less than 10 minutes, which means you'll be on your way and out the door in no time. Those ten minutes are a small price to pay to prevent a litany of potential health issues.

Many people are resistant to the idea of applying any kind of skincare products, but wrinkles, blemishes, and unhealthy skin can appear if you're not careful. Take a few minutes every day to pamper yourself and you'll notice the difference in your skin.

47

STOP HOARDING STUFF

If you've lived in your home for any period of time, chances are that you've accumulated quite a bit of stuff. Whether that's knickknacks from local garage sales, fitness equipment that you thought you would use, or a collection of cereal boxes that you swore would be worth a fortune someday, we all have things lying around that we could do without.

At some point your life (if it hasn't happened already), you look around and start to question the usefulness of all these items. There will be a certain emotional pull that will try to get you to keep it no matter the cost. However, there is a very real and liberating feeling that comes from purging your life of unnecessary items. It'll make you feel fuller, more flexible, and somehow *younger*. You'll be less connected to the items that you have and more connected to the things that you *want* to have. That mindset shift creates a world of difference.

The simplest way to purge your life from these items, assuming that you're emotionally ready, is to form three different piles: trash, donate, and sell. Round up everything in your life that you know nobody else needs and throw it in the dumpster. Then, collect a bunch of items that you think you can make some money from and put those in storage boxes to get ready for a garage sale. Finally, take whatever is left — along with the items that don't sell — and head down to your local thrift store. If it's a nonprofit, make sure that you get a donation slip to claim these items later on your taxes.

If you're not very comfortable with the idea of having a garage sale (and many people aren't) then see if you can sell those items online through eBay or some other outlet. Craigslist and Facebook marketplaces can help you get rid of all that stuff by selling it to people who are local. Usually, you will get a lot more than you would at a garage sale anyway. Moreover, if you select local pickup, the only thing left to do is put it on your front porch for somebody to grab. It couldn't be easier.

I understand that not everybody is ready for a purge, and please don't think that I'm suggesting that you need to get rid of every single thing that you own and become a minimalist (although there's nothing wrong with that). I'm saying that getting rid of some of the unnecessary items that have been cluttering up your life and your mind can be removed with minimal pain.

It's as simple as ripping off a Band-Aid. Once it's gone, you'll barely remember what it was that you had in the first place. You'll also start to notice the items in your life that you may have overlooked.

48

SAVE MONEY

Many people consider their forties and fifties to be the apex of their earning power. After all, it's when you have the most experience and the most leverage. You've likely also attained a certain rank inside of a company or industry that allows you to command the most money. While there will always be people coming in behind you who will do the job for cheaper, a lot of employers really appreciate having people around them that they can trust and that they've worked with for years. They're willing to pay extra to keep you by their side.

Along with that increase in earning power comes an increased desire to spend more money. Without contradicting the earlier advice to splurge on an item you really, really want, you should also be looking to save as much money as possible. The compounding interest that you can have from this point forward may not be as much as it was when you're in your twenties, but there's still a lot of years left for you to invest and reap the financial rewards of a good financial strategy. At this point in your life, you should also have quite a few of your debts paid off, so take advantage of that flexibility by setting aside more money for later years.

The fact that you're making more money now than you probably will at any other point your life may be disheartening to some, but we have to look at it realistically and not shut our eyes to the reality of what's in front of us. Sure, you may be able to work for another 20 or 30 years, but even if you are able to, would you want to? I guarantee you won't remember a lot of the superficial things that you wanted when you're 70. Instead, you'll be happy that you set aside some of that money to save up for an earlier retirement. I've met so many people who neglected their savings account at this point in their lives only to regret it later.

Some people decide to skate into their retirement on a wing and a prayer, hoping that Social Security and the 401(k) that their employer has been matching all these years will be enough (and it might be). However, it's always better to be overprepared than not prepared enough. At the very least, taking charge of your savings and investments now will help you approach your retirement day with confidence, joy, and optimism. There's peace in knowing that you not only have the money that you need to survive, but also enough for all of the things that you've always wanted to do.

49

LEARN ABOUT TECHNOLOGY

Like it or not, technology is here to stay. The world is moving at an accelerated pace, and people are finding faster, easier, cheaper, and more efficient ways to accomplish everyday tasks. Rather than rail against this technology and drone on and on about the way things "used to be," embrace it instead. While new technology can be confusing and overwhelming, a lot of it is genuinely designed to make our lives better. Looking into some of these systems can make for a very interesting hobby.

This doesn't mean that you need to be on TikTok (as a matter of fact, I would argue *against* it, if for no other reason than it can dominate your time). But you should still take some time to familiarize yourself with major social media networks, internet terms, and other burgeoning technologies like smart homes and autonomous cars. Many of these devices are making lives much simpler. This efficiency results in more time spent on things that really do matter, such as living your everyday life. A lot of people complain against these devices out of a sense of tradition and claim that the way that things have always been done is better. Not only is that shortsighted, it's also unnecessary.

Talk to any grandmother who has recently found the joy of being able to FaceTime their granddaughter with an iPad or a retired landscaper who marvels at the autonomous drone that mows their lawn every single morning before he's even up. You'll see just how much of a difference these technologies can make.

Even something like security systems have made huge strides in recent years. You used to have to pay a professional to hardwire your house with all sorts of gadgets, then route them to a central mainframe to operate. These days, you can have a professional security system that monitors smoke, carbon monoxide, and other noxious gases in addition to providing 24/7 security services. It's really astounding what kind of security systems are available now. Many can be installed by just about anyone in less than a few hours.

50

CONSIDER
YOUR LEGACY

Have you ever wondered what people will think about you when you're gone? I realize that 50 isn't nearly the end of your life (not even close) but legacies aren't built in a day. You shouldn't wait decades before you start to consider what yours will be. Memories you make with your family, causes you support, and even everyday interactions define who you are and how people will remember you.

I've seen far too many people try to manufacture a legacy out of thin air based on someone they never really wanted to be in the first place. Some will start donating to charity because they want to be thought of as a kind and hospitable person. While that's noble of them, you don't need to spend 40 hours a week working with Habitat for Humanity to cement who you are in people's minds. Usually, spending a few hours a week with people in your home, visiting hospitals, and frequenting nursing homes will make a ton of difference in people's lives.

Maybe you're someone who wants to be known as an innovator. You've always thought of yourself as an inventor, tinkering around with devices in your garage after work. Why not see if you can patent one or two of those? If you're really lucky, maybe a company will pick them up and pay you royalties for a period of time. It's possible!

The main argument here is that it's never too late to consider who you are or what kind of mark you'll make on the world. Use these "micro interactions" that you have with people on an everyday basis and consider how your life folds into the larger story of the universe. Were you a mentor to somebody? Did you start a nonprofit or work for one that you're proud of? Did you create a piece of art that people will cherish for generations? All of these things add up to the idea that people have of you. Start thinking about ways that you can work on something that will outlive even you.

It seems gloomy to end a book that's about turning 50 with a chapter on considering your legacy once you're gone, but this is truly the thing that will be eternal on this Earth. The rest of the items on this list may help you enjoy the second half your life, but this is the one that will allow your name to live on for generation after generation. It's the only real fountain of youth that is available to us, and it's easier than we might think to obtain.

If you're having a hard time considering your legacy, I would encourage you to think about ways that you can serve other people. While having a star on the Hollywood Walk of Fame is nice, people tend to remember those who helped them along the way instead. It truly is one of the great paradoxes of our time that in serving others, we also serve ourselves. Along the way, we might even establish a legacy that will live on for years to come.

Regardless of what you want to be known for, it's never too late to get started.

Made in United States
Orlando, FL
06 February 2022

14488449R00067